Original title:
Jubilant Leaves Across the Goblin Marsh

Author: Paula Raudsepp
ISBN HARDBACK: 978-1-80559-108-5
ISBN PAPERBACK: 978-1-80559-607-3

Festivity Dressed in Nature's Array

Colors dance in leafy sway,
Sunlight gleams through branches play.
Petals twirl, a fragrant bliss,
Nature calls, we can't resist.

Streamlets laugh with sparkling glee,
Bees and butterflies roam free.
Joyful songs from birds arise,
Echoing beneath blue skies.

Swaying grasses, soft and bright,
Bathe in warm, golden light.
In this tapestry so grand,
We hold life within our hand.

Crisp autumn whispers wait to show,
Sapphire skies, the first snow's glow.
Festivities in hues so rare,
We celebrate, in nature's care.

The Green Ballad of Woodland Wonders

Deep in woodland, secrets hum,
Gentle echoes, where dreams come.
Mossy carpets welcome all,
Nature's whispers, soft and small.

Trees stand tall with stories old,
Guardians of the tales retold.
Each rustling leaf a note of grace,
Dancing shadows in this place.

Beneath the canopies of green,
Life unfolds, serene, unseen.
Frogs in chorus, crickets play,
A symphony through night and day.

Glade's embrace, where wonders dwell,
Nature speaks, a soothing spell.
Wandering hearts find their tune,
In the bright embrace of June.

Enigma and Elation in Mossy Realms

In the heart of vibrant green,
Mysteries that lie unseen.
Moss envelops ancient bark,
Whispers soft, igniting spark.

Sunbeams filter, a silver show,
In this realm, dreams ebb and flow.
Ferns unfurl, secrets shared,
A language only few have dared.

Rustling winds through branches call,
Echoing in the forest hall.
Elation glints in dew-soaked dawn,
Nature's magic, softly drawn.

Each step veils a hidden dance,
Life's enigma, wild romance.
In mossy realms where whispers bloom,
Hearts entwine in nature's womb.

Embrace of the Glistening Fables

Stars alight, the night is clear,
Glistening tales we hold dear.
Moonlit paths guide gentle souls,
Whispers weave through evening's rolls.

As shadows stretch across the glade,
Time stands still, all worries fade.
Fables carved in the night's embrace,
Stories linger in this space.

Fireflies dance in twinkling flight,
Guiding dreamers through the night.
Nature's glow, a soft refrain,
In the silence, joy remains.

Embrace the night, let spirits soar,
In the magic, we explore.
With every heartbeat, tales we share,
In glistening fables, we lay bare.

Whispers of the Wooded Revelry

In the hush where shadows blend,
The trees their secrets share,
Voices dance upon the wind,
Inviting all who dare.

Moonlight drapes a silver sheet,
Upon the forest floor,
Rustling leaves beneath my feet,
Echo dreams of yore.

Mushrooms glow in twilight's grace,
Flickering as they sway,
Each step leading to a place,
Where night becomes the day.

Crickets chirp a lullaby,
Bats weave through the night air,
Laughter lifts up to the sky,
With joy beyond compare.

In this realm of whispered songs,
A magic pure and free,
Wooded revels gently throngs,
Inviting you and me.

The Frolic of Emerald Fronds

Beneath the canopy so green,
Where sunlight filters rare,
Frogs leap high in joyful scene,
Chasing dreams without a care.

Dew-kissed ferns in breezes twirl,
As laughter rides the stream,
Nature's gems in graceful swirl,
Awake in vivid dream.

Squirrels scamper, tails aflame,
Through branches soft and light,
Each moment sings a wild name,
As day turns into night.

Quiet whispers, breezes soft,
Stir the panicles high,
In the dance of elements oft,
The forest hums a sigh.

Here in the embrace of greens,
Life flows in every bay,
The frolic of the fronds, it seems,
Is where the spirits play.

Enchantment in the Misty Glade

In the glade where vapors rise,
Misty veils wrap the ground,
Underneath the cloudy skies,
Magic whispers all around.

Silence reigns, yet secrets bloom,
Petals twirl in soft delight,
Every shadow holds a room,
Where dreams peek into night.

Fairy lights blink, twinkle bright,
Guiding lost souls that roam,
Through the mist, they find their flight,
Welcoming them back home.

Crickets sing their lullabies,
Stars emerge, a distant gleam,
In this space, where magic lies,
We awaken to the dream.

Here enchantment finds its grace,
While time drifts like the breeze,
In the misty glade's embrace,
Hearts become forever free.

Merriment in the Faery Thicket

In thickets dense with dreams and glee,
Where faeries flit and play,
Laughter echoes, wild and free,
In the dusk of fading day.

Glowing orbs, they dance above,
Casting warmth on every face,
In this realm of joy and love,
Every heart finds its place.

Mushroom rings a lively stage,
Where spirits leap and twirl,
In the faery thicket's cage,
Every moment's a whirl.

Glimmers of light weave in and out,
Through the branches, soft and low,
Enchanted whispers, without a doubt,
Guide the wanderers below.

Merriment spills from every nook,
Sunset wraps in soft embrace,
In this playful, secret book,
We find a wondrous space.

Chromatic Joy in the Misty Canopy

Colors dance in morning light,
A symphony of hues so bright.
Leaves whisper songs of silver dew,
In this mist the world feels new.

Petals drop like fragrant dreams,
Nature's art in sunlit beams.
Joyful breezes swirl around,
In this magic, peace is found.

Breezes carry secrets sweet,
Every corner begs to greet.
Vibrant life beneath the sky,
Where the wildflowers never die.

With every glance, a new delight,
Chromatic wonders banish night.
Underneath the verdant shade,
Moments cherished, never fade.

Lose yourself in colors grand,
In this lush, enchanted land.
Every shade a song of glee,
In the mist, we are set free.

Radiant Whispers Beneath the Boughs

Gentle murmurs fill the air,
Beneath the boughs, without a care.
Radiance spills through tangled leaves,
Nature's hand, the heart believes.

With every breath, a tale unfolds,
Of ancient roots and secrets told.
Sunlight filters through the trees,
Each moment dances on the breeze.

Soft shadows play on forest floor,
Where every step reveals much more.
Whispers echo through the glade,
In the silence, memories fade.

Glowing beams escape the crown,
Wrapping all in nature's gown.
Here under the leafy dome,
We find solace, a sacred home.

Thus we wander, hearts in tune,
With radiant whispers, morning's boon.
Beneath the boughs, time drifts away,
In this haven, we choose to stay.

Frolics Under the Shady Canopy

In the shade where laughter rings,
Hidden joys that nature brings.
Beneath the branches, we align,
Frolics dance, our spirits shine.

Children chase the fluttering light,
Through the trees, in pure delight.
Leaves giggle as they twist and sway,
Inviting dreams to come and play.

Each step echoes in the green,
Where the sun and shadows blend.
Underneath this leafy shield,
Every moment feels revealed.

Joy rushes with the babbling brook,
At every nook, a storybook.
We weave tales of wild endeavor,
In this realm, we're young forever.

With laughter ringing, we are free,
Frolics under the grand oak tree.
Memories spun in nature's thread,
In shady canopies, we tread.

The Magic of Whirling Green Vignettes

In the breeze, the stories weave,
Whirling greens, a dance to believe.
Each vignette, a soft embrace,
Where every glance finds a trace.

Nature paints in vibrant strokes,
Echoing the call of folks.
Through emerald twists, we glide along,
A journey bound for hearts so strong.

Every leaf, a fleeting glance,
Each shadow holds a secret dance.
Moments captured in a frame,
In this tapestry, never the same.

Around the trees, our laughter rings,
In the magic that freedom brings.
Whirling light, a playful touch,
In this haven, we love so much.

The world beyond feels far away,
In these vignettes, we choose to stay.
Spinning tales of vibrant cheer,
In nature's heart, our paths are clear.

The Sassy Caper of Twisted Roots

In the woods where shadows dance,
Sassy whispers weave a chance,
Twisted roots with secrets bold,
Adventure waits, the tale is told.

A flick of light, a teasing breeze,
Giddy hearts beneath the trees,
Nature's charm, a playful plight,
Twisted paths lead to delight.

Giggling fairies spin and twirl,
Magic swirls, a joyous whirl,
Every step, a jolly romp,
In the undergrowth, they clomp.

Roots entangle, snags abound,
Yet the laughter knows no bound,
In this caper wild and free,
Twisted roots, our jubilee.

So join the sassy, spirited chase,
In the woods, find your place,
Among the twisted, laugh and play,
Let the roots guide your way.

Starlit Mirth in the Goblins' Domain

In the glen where goblins dwell,
Starlit mirth rings like a bell,
Laughter echoes through the night,
Twinkling eyes, a magical sight.

Gathered round the bonfire's glow,
Mischievous secrets start to flow,
With every jest, the night grows bright,
Goblins dance in pure delight.

Crickets sing a soothing tune,
Underneath the silver moon,
Tiny boots tap to the beat,
In this realm, all joys repeat.

Filled with mischief, love, and cheer,
The goblins laugh, there's nothing to fear,
Together they weave a night so fine,
Where starlit mirth and spirits shine.

As dawn approaches, shadows fade,
But in their hearts, the joy's not swayed,
In the goblins' domain so grand,
Starlit mirth forever stands.

Fermenting Joy in the Leafy Labyrinth

In a labyrinth of verdant delight,
Where leaves embrace from morning to night,
Joy ferments in the gentle sway,
Nature's whims lead us astray.

Sunlight filters through the green,
Painting dreams yet unseen,
Every twist, a story unfolds,
In the leafy heart, adventure molds.

Petals flutter, laughter sprouts,
In every corner, joy shouts,
Whispers of joy fill the air,
In this maze, we have no care.

Breath of earth, a fragrant cheer,
With each moment, love draws near,
In the dance of life, we roam,
The leafy labyrinth feels like home.

As night descends with a gentle sigh,
We hold the joy, we fly high,
In this haven, forever stay,
Fermenting love, come what may.

Sounds of Celebration in Tattered Petals

In a garden worn yet bright,
Tattered petals catch the light,
Sounds of joy begin to rise,
Through the air, sweet music flies.

Humming bees and soft, sweet chimes,
Echo laughter, rhythm of times,
Dancing hearts upon the breeze,
In this haven, spirits tease.

Colors swirl in joyous flow,
Celebration steals the show,
Every bloom sings a refrain,
In tattered petals, joy remains.

With weary blooms, the beauty stays,
In every crevice, love displays,
The sounds of life, a vibrant song,
In this garden, we belong.

So let the petals tap and sway,
With every voice, we greet the day,
In sounds of joy, forever leap,
In the heart of petals, joy runs deep.

Echoes of Joy Amidst the Canopied Chaos

In dappled light, they dance and play,
Laughter flows like a gentle stream.
Joyful whispers ride on the breeze,
Where chaos fades, and hearts can dream.

Beneath the arch of emerald leaves,
Nature's symphony starts to swell.
Every heartbeat sings a promise,
In this haven, all is well.

The sunlight breaks through woven greens,
Crafting patterns on earthy floors.
Echoes of joy ripple through time,
In this space, the spirit soars.

Together they weave tales anew,
In chorus with the rustling light.
Moments captured, free and bright,
In the chaos, pure delight.

As twilight wraps the world in gold,
The laughter fades, but memories stay.
In every heart, this joy resides,
Whispering soft, in dreams, they play.

The Happy Lilt of Rustling Leaves

Breezes tease the trees to sway,
Rustling leaves in joyous song.
Each whisper tells of summer's grace,
Where hearts and nature both belong.

Sunlight glimmers, shadows dance,
A playful tune in woodland air.
Nature hums a lilting sound,
A harmony beyond compare.

Every turn, a new delight,
In the canopy's soft embrace.
The rustling leaves with laughter call,
A melody of love and grace.

Around each corner, secrets spin,
As whispers flit from branch to bough.
The happy lilt of rustling leaves,
Is life's sweet serenade right now.

At dusk, the song begins to fade,
Yet echoes linger in our minds.
The leaves continue their gentle sway,
In every heart, their joy combines.

Gleeful Secrets Among the Foliage

In the heart of the emerald thicket,
Gleeful secrets softly run.
Whispers of joy sneak through the leaves,
Beneath the glow of the setting sun.

Each branch a story waiting to tell,
Of laughter shared in the sunlight's gleam.
Dancing shadows play a game of hide,
As nature unfolds her sweetest dream.

The rustling ferns keep quiet watch,
On the giggles of birds overhead.
In the soft embrace of the forest deep,
Where every leaf holds a tale unsaid.

A world alive with a gentle hum,
The breeze carries laughter through the trees.
Gleeful secrets, cherished and bright,
In the canopy's arms, we find our ease.

As night descends, wishes twinkle too,
In the stillness, secrets softly call.
Amongst the foliage, we find our hearts,
In the dance of shadows, we lose it all.

Mischievous Melodies in Woodland Nooks

In hidden glades where shadows play,
Mischievous melodies take flight.
Whispers of laughter, soft and sweet,
Echoing through the cloak of night.

With every rustle, a tune unfolds,
As creatures frolic in secret glee.
The forest hums a lively beat,
In nooks where joy is wild and free.

Branches sway with a playful touch,
While crickets sing their evening hymn.
Nature's choir is alive tonight,
As stars above begin to brim.

Twinkling eyes in the twilight's glow,
Watch as the woodland brims with cheer.
Mischievous melodies linger long,
Entwining hearts with joy so dear.

As dawn breaks with whispered sighs,
The notes of laughter slowly fade.
Yet echoes linger in the dawn,
In every nook, true joy is made.

Rejoicing in the Gloomy Thicket

In shadows deep, where sorrows blend,
The laughter whispers, hopes ascend.
Each secret nook, a dream unfurls,
In the thicket's heart, joy twirls.

Beneath the leaves, a solace found,
In every rustle, life's sweet sound.
Misty breaths, the dawn ignites,
Gloom transforms, embracing lights.

Among twisted roots, we spin and sway,
Nature's dance guides the way.
With every step, old fears depart,
A melody blooms in every heart.

The thicket's gloom, a soft embrace,
Hiding secrets, sheltering grace.
Through tangled paths, we wander free,
In darkness, we find harmony.

Joy intertwines with shadows near,
Each moment savored, stripped of fear.
Rejoicing here, in twilight's glow,
The thicket's love will ever grow.

Spirited Swirls in the Foliate Glade

Leaves dance wildly, in the breeze,
Spirited swirls amongst the trees.
Whispers of magic fill the air,
In the glade, hope's sometimes rare.

Sunlight flickers, shadows play,
Gentle spirits guide the way.
Colors burst, a vivid sight,
Foliate glade, a pure delight.

Every branch tells tales untold,
Of brave and bold, and hearts of gold.
In the rustle, laughter rings,
Nature shares her countless things.

Winds of fortune, laugh and soar,
Embracing all, from shore to shore.
Magic stirs in every swell,
In the glade, we weave our spell.

Here we gather, souls entwined,
With whispered dreams, all finely lined.
In swirls of joy, we find our pace,
In the glade's warm embrace, we trace.

Glittering Bliss Within the Burrows

Deep in the earth, where shadows gleam,
Glittering bliss wraps all in dream.
Burrows filled with treasures rare,
Life's sweet secrets, hidden there.

Winding paths of earthen lore,
Whispering winds through every door.
Softly glows the amber light,
Guiding hearts through velvet night.

Creatures stir in twilight's glow,
Dancing where the starlings flow.
Blissful moments, stolen away,
In burrows deep, we long to stay.

In silence, sighs of comfort bloom,
Nestled close in earthen room.
Every heartbeat sings a tune,
Beneath the watchful, silver moon.

Here in burrows, laughter reigns,
A treasure trove, joy unchains.
Through glittering paths, we roam at will,
In blissful caves, our hearts we fill.

A Feast of Fables Underneath the Stars

Beneath the stars, where stories blend,
A feast of fables, magic bends.
Whispers float on night's cool breath,
Each tale woven, a dance with death.

Gathered 'round, the fire burns bright,
Casting shadows, igniting night.
With every word, new worlds arise,
Fables glow beneath the skies.

Hear the tales of love and woe,
In moonlit gleam, emotions flow.
Every voice, a heart unveiled,
In shared stories, we are hailed.

Nibbles shared from hands of friends,
Each laughter echoes, never ends.
The feast continues, bonds unite,
Underneath the stars, pure delight.

As constellations spin their lore,
In fables told, we crave for more.
A banquet rich with dreams and scars,
We revel deeply, beneath the stars.

Gleeful Spirits Treading Softly

Whispers of laughter fill the air,
Tiny footsteps dancing here and there.
Joyful hearts spin in sweet delight,
Under the glow of the moonlight.

Fields of wildflowers sway and bend,
Nature's canvas, where dreams extend.
With every twirl, the world feels bright,
Gleeful spirits paint the night.

In the stillness, secrets unfold,
Stories of wonder, treasures untold.
Breeze carries tunes from afar,
Echoing under the evening star.

Gentle shadows play on the ground,
Each soft step, a magical sound.
Together they weave a tapestry,
Of joy and love, pure energy.

In laughter's embrace, they find their way,
Crafting memories that forever stay.
With hearts unburdened, they roam free,
Gleeful spirits, in harmony.

Nature's Heartbeat in Dappled Light

Sunlight filters through the trees,
Kissing leaves with tender ease.
In the quiet, life takes its flight,
Nature pulses with pure delight.

Birds sing sweetly, notes entwined,
In the hush, peace is defined.
Every rustle, a lover's sigh,
Underneath the painted sky.

Rivers murmur a soothing song,
Carrying whispers that drift along.
With each ripple, secrets ignite,
Nature's heartbeat, day and night.

Dappled shadows dance and play,
Painting brief moments, come what may.
In this canvas, we find our place,
Wrapped in beauty, a warm embrace.

The wind caresses, a gentle guide,
Through valleys deep and mountains wide.
Together we wander, hearts so light,
In nature's embrace, everything's right.

The Merry Tune of Swamp Dancers

Amidst the reeds, a rhythm flows,
Where laughter mingles with the crows.
Frogs keep time with their croaking cheer,
Swamp dancers gather, bringing near.

Moonbeams shimmer on the water's face,
Inviting all to join the race.
Beneath the stars, their spirits soar,
Moving to nature's vibrant roar.

In muddy shoes, they twirl and spin,
With every step, they let joy in.
Flickering fireflies illuminate the night,
Guiding their feet in pure delight.

Swamp's embrace, a stage divine,
Every heart beats in perfect line.
With laughter echoing through the air,
It's magic woven everywhere.

In this haven, where freedom reigns,
They dance away all worldly pains.
The merry tune rings warm and clear,
In the swamp, they have no fear.

Bewitched Blossoms Under Starry Skies

In twilight's hush, the flowers bloom,
Whispers of magic scent the room.
Under starlight, colors gleam,
Awakening wonder, like a dream.

Petals shimmer in the cool night air,
Nurtured by moonlight, delicate care.
Each blossom sways with secret grace,
In nature's dance, they find their place.

Softly the breeze carries their song,
Inviting all to join along.
Bewitched by beauty, the night unfolds,
Stories of love in the petals told.

Cascades of fragrance fill the sky,
As night creatures quietly pass by.
Every glance is a spellbound kiss,
In the garden of moments, pure bliss.

To wander here is to touch the divine,
Where every star seems to brightly shine.
Under the heavens, hearts intertwine,
Bewitched blossoms, forever shine.

The Revelers in Feathery Shrouds

In twilight's glow, they dance with grace,
A flurry of colors, a soft embrace.
With whispers of secrets, the night unfurls,
Their laughter blooms like petals in swirls.

Clad in feathers, bright and bold,
Stories of old, in movements told.
Amidst the stars, they float on air,
In revels of dreams, they have a care.

Moonlit paths and glistening dew,
The nightingale sings, a harmonic hue.
In circles they form, a joyful sight,
Bound by the magic of fading light.

With every twirl, a tale begins,
Of fate and fortune, of losses and wins.
They weave the night in whimsical charms,
Wrapped in splendors, their spirits warm.

As morning breaks, the shadows flee,
Leaving mere whispers of what used to be.
Yet in their hearts, the essence remains,
A dance eternal, in soft refrains.

Fantasies Woven in Verdant Serenade

In forests deep, where silence reigns,
Whispers of dreams in the gentle rains.
Emerald canopies shelter the heart,
Nature's embrace, a world set apart.

With every leaf, a story unfurls,
Of fae and creatures, in daylight swirls.
The rivers hum with secrets untold,
Reflections of glories from ages of old.

Petals brush softly against the skin,
As melodies drift like a soft violin.
In harmony's arms, the echoes play,
Fantasies bloom, they linger and sway.

The sun slips low, casting shadows long,
Nature rejoices in a vibrant song.
With each raindrop, new tales arise,
In verdant serenades beneath the skies.

So lay your heart on the mossy ground,
Listen closely to the dreams that abound.
In whispers and rustles, they softly call,
In this tapestry of life, we find our all.

The Cheerful Conclave of Twig and Leaf

Gathered 'round, the twigs unite,
A conclave held in the soft twilight.
Leaves interlace in a friendly throng,
Their chatter mingles like a joyous song.

Each twig a tale of seasons past,
Of storms endured and shadows cast.
The leaves recall the sun's warm rays,
Each whisper a memory that gently stays.

With dewdrops glistening like morning dreams,
They share their secrets in rippling streams.
Their laughter spills like the song of birds,
In a symphony woven with gentle words.

As night descends, they sway and bend,
In every rustle, new messages send.
The moon nods down with a knowing smile,
A witness to joy that stretches a mile.

Together they stand, steadfast and free,
In nature's embrace, where spirits agree.
Through seasons of change, they rise and fall,
The cheerful conclave, the heart of it all.

Harmonies of the Mischievous Fae

In shadows cast by the silver moonlight,
Mischievous fae twinkle with delight.
Their laughter rings in the midnight air,
Playing tricks with a deft, witty flair.

With wings aglow, they flit and tease,
Whirling around the ancient trees.
They sprinkle laughter on waning dreams,
In a world alive with giggling beams.

Lost in the dance of the twilight hour,
Their playful spirits hold endless power.
Echoes of joy weave through the night,
As they spin and twirl, pure hearts take flight.

With every flutter of gossamer grace,
They invite us all to this enchanted place.
In mischief and mirth, they sing their song,
Harmonies swell, where all belong.

So heed the whispers of twilight's call,
Join in their revels, let your spirit enthrall.
For in their laughter and playful glee,
Lies the magic of all that can be.

Euphoria of Nature's Secret Troupe

In whispers soft, the leaves converse,
A dance unfolds, a vibrant verse.
The breeze carries tales untold,
Nature's secrets, rich and bold.

Beneath the boughs, the shadows play,
Gentle laughter, a bright bouquet.
Colors twirl in morning light,
Euphoria blooms, pure delight.

Fluttering wings, a symphony,
In harmony with each green tree.
The world awakens, spirited and free,
In nature's magic, unity.

The river hums a soothing song,
Its melody, where we belong.
The earth rejoices, a timeless sound,
In secret troves, joy is found.

In twilight's glow, the dance will cease,
As day surrenders, granting peace.
Yet in the dark, dreams softly bloom,
In nature's heart, we find our room.

Harmony of the Singing Rivermoss

Moss carpets banks where waters glint,
A gentle song, the edges hint.
The currents weave through emerald strands,
Nature's voice, in soft commands.

Ripples echo secrets shared,
In this realm, all hearts are bared.
Each droplet sings of tales long past,
In harmony, their shadows cast.

Sunlight dances on the stream,
Creating visions, like a dream.
Together, flora sways and bows,
In harmony, the river vows.

The rush of water, pure and free,
A melody of eternity.
With every flow, a new refrain,
In rivermoss, we find our gain.

As twilight hushes day to night,
The singing softly dims its light.
But in our souls, the echoes stay,
In harmony, we'll find our way.

Leaves in Laughter's Leap

Leaves tumble down in joyous flight,
A dance of color, pure delight.
They laugh and spiral, play and tease,
In the gentle sway of autumn's breeze.

Golden whispers fill the air,
Nature's chorus, everywhere.
Each leaf a story, bright and bold,
In laughter's leap, our hearts unfold.

Branches sway with playful grace,
Welcoming change, a warm embrace.
In every rustle, joy is found,
In nature's rhythm, we are bound.

The sunlight kisses every hue,
As shadows dance, and time is new.
The world, a canvas, painted free,
In laughter's leap, we learn to be.

As dusk approaches, light will fade,
Yet in our hearts, the joy will stay.
Leaves will return, in cycles deep,
In laughter's leap, our dreams we keep.

The Sway of Mirthful Tides

Waves kiss the shore in a playful way,
The tides sing songs of a glorious day.
With every surge, they dance and glide,
In mirthful rhythm, they turn the tide.

Seagulls cry, their laughter bright,
Chasing waves in the morning light.
The ocean's breath, a lullaby,
In every splash, dreams soar high.

Sands beneath our feet feel warm,
A soothing touch, nature's charm.
Children build their castles wide,
In the sway of the joyous tide.

Evening comes, the sun dips low,
Colors blend in a radiant show.
The horizon hums a tranquil verse,
In mirthful tides, we converse.

As stars emerge in the deep blue sea,
Waves whisper secrets, wild and free.
Each heartbeat echoes, never hides,
In the sway of mirthful tides.

Vaudeville of the Verdant

In the glade where shadows play,
Leaves twirl lightly, bright and gay.
Breezes whisper, secrets share,
Nature's stage is rich and rare.

Sunlight glimmers, patterns weave,
Every turn's a chance to believe.
Floral voices rise and burst,
As all around, the songs immerse.

Colors clash in vibrant cheer,
A motley crew of joy draws near.
Dancers twirl on emerald grass,
In this show, time seems to pass.

With every step, the heart will leap,
Memories form, laughter deep.
Underneath the ancient trees,
Life's great humor flows with ease.

Curtains close with twilight's call,
For now, we bid farewell to all.
Yet in dreams, the dances stay,
Vaudeville alive, come what may.

Laughter Carried on the Wind's Breath

Laughter floats on gentle air,
Echoing without a care.
Tickling leaves with every tease,
Soft as whispers in the breeze.

Chirping birds join in the fun,
Bathed in warm and golden sun.
Every giggle finds its way,
In the dance of light and play.

Clouds drift by, a playful crew,
Casting shadows, shaping blue.
While the sun shines down so bright,
Joyful spirits take to flight.

Bubbles rise in laughter's wake,
Carried forth by every shake.
As the world spins, twirls around,
Every heart's melody found.

In this symphony of cheer,
Moments cherished, held so near.
The wind's breath whispers a song,
In our hearts, where it belongs.

The Elysian Dance of Pine Needles

Beneath the pines, a soft lament,
In green embrace, our hearts content.
With every sway, the needles fall,
Nature's rhythm, a soothing call.

In twilight's glow, shadows play,
Chasing dreams where spirits stay.
Rustling whispers guide the way,
Through the woods where fairies stray.

Moonlight weaves a silver thread,
As creatures dance, the magic spread.
Pine-scented air, a soothing balm,
In this haven, all is calm.

Elysian beats in every heart,
Nature's beauty, a work of art.
Caught in the shimmer of the trees,
In this moment, the soul sees.

Echoes linger, softly sway,
As night unfolds its grand display.
In the dance of needles twined,
Elysian dreams, forever lined.

Sundrenched Joy in the Shrouded Paths

Through tangled trails where shadows creep,
Sundrenched joy, awake from sleep.
Golden rays break through the veil,
Lighting up the hidden trail.

Flowers bloom with colors bright,
Life emerges in pure delight.
Every step a fresh surprise,
Nature's wonders feast the eyes.

Gentle caress of sunlit beams,
Whispers woven in our dreams.
Joy weaves through each winding turn,
In the heart, a fire burns.

Birds above in joyful flight,
Live the song of morning light.
With every note that fills the air,
Hope and laughter, everywhere.

Paths may twist and turn around,
But in each corner, joy is found.
Sundrenched moments brightly blend,
In fading light, our spirits mend.

Wild Revelry Under the Canopy Stars

Beneath the stars, we dance and sing,
The night alive with joy we bring.
The rustling leaves join in our fight,
As laughter echoes through the night.

We sway beneath the ancient trees,
With whispers carried by the breeze.
The moon, our guide, shines soft and bright,
Illuminating our hearts' delight.

In shadows deep, our spirits play,
As we embrace the wild array.
With every twirl, we feel the spark,
Igniting love within the dark.

The canopy holds secrets vast,
In stories of the ones who passed.
But here we are, alive and free,
In wild revelry, just you and me.

The Joyous Palette of Earth's Whimsy

Colors dance on the canvas of Earth,
Each shade reveals its quiet worth.
From blossoms bright to skies so clear,
Nature's brush brings forth our cheer.

In fields of gold, we laugh and prance,
With every step, we join the dance.
The fragrance lifts our spirits high,
As butterflies flit gently by.

Rivers shimmer in joyful glee,
Reflecting all the life we see.
The palette swirls in endless flow,
With vibrant tales the flowers show.

Together, we paint the day's best hue,
In every stroke, my heart finds you.
With joy as bright as morning's glow,
We wander where the wild things grow.

Whirling Spirits and Dappled Delight

In sunlight's dance, the shadows play,
Whirling spirits guide our way.
Dappled light upon the ground,
In nature's arms, our peace is found.

Through forests thick, we move with grace,
As nature smiles on our wild chase.
The melodies of life resound,
In every heartbeat, love is found.

With twinkling eyes, we spin around,
In joyous circles, we are bound.
Each moment cherished, soft and bright,
We lose ourselves in pure delight.

The echoes of our laughter rise,
Like fleeting dreams that touch the skies.
Connected with the world so grand,
In whirling joy, together we stand.

The Leafy Laughter in Silvery Streams

By the brook where the willows weep,
Leafy laughter stirs from sleep.
Ripples dance, reflecting light,
As nature's joy takes flight.

The gentle breeze sings through the trees,
Carries whispers on the ease.
Each leaf a note, a joyful sound,
In harmony, we are bound.

Crickets share their evening song,
As shadows stretch and grow strong.
With every splash and every gleam,
We run wild, lost in dream.

In the glade, we skip and play,
With laughter bright as light of day.
The silvery streams our hearts embrace,
In nature's arms, we find our place.

Glee of the Gnarled Branches

In twilight's whisper, secrets flow,
Gnarled branches dance, in shadows they glow.
Each twist a tale, old and profound,
Roots intertwined deep in the ground.

Leaves rustle softly, a playful song,
Memories linger, where they belong.
The wind laughs gently, a light-hearted tease,
Nature's embrace, puts the heart at ease.

Beneath the canopy, dreams take flight,
Dancing in patterns, pure delight.
A symphony plays in the air so sweet,
Gnarled branches sway, the rhythm's heartbeat.

Fingers of twilight stretch and weave,
Through tangled limbs, where spirits believe.
The night wraps around with a tender sigh,
In the glee of branches, we learn to fly.

Moonlight kisses the bark, soft and pure,
As night unfolds, its magic's allure.
In the gnarled embrace, we find our way,
Where shadows dance, and night turns to day.

The Mirthful Glimmer of Forest Dew

In morning's blush, the forest wakes,
Dewdrops glimmer, like gentle flakes.
Mirthful jewels on leaves they rest,
A sparkling crown on nature's vest.

Soft whispers echo through the trees,
As sunlight tumbles, a playful breeze.
Each droplet shines, a tiny sun,
Reflecting joy where all begun.

Tiny worlds within each sphere,
A glimpse of magic, crystal clear.
In every glimmer, stories unfurl,
Nature's laughter in a twirling whirl.

The path adorned with a shimmering coat,
As if the earth had spun and wrote.
In this wonder, the heart can dance,
Embracing the moment, a fleeting chance.

The sun climbs high, the dew will fade,
Yet in our hearts, the memory stayed.
Of forest gleams and laughter's hue,
In every step, the dew renews.

Secrets Unveiled in the Leafy Ball

Beneath the boughs where shadows creep,
A leafy ball holds secrets deep.
Whispers linger in the air,
Stories woven, a tale to share.

The rustling leaves sigh soft and low,
As if they know what we don't show.
Each flutter hides a world untold,
In hues of green and threads of gold.

In dappled light, the fables breath,
Echoing life, from birth to death.
A dance of thoughts in the gentle sway,
Where light and dark converge and play.

The twilight beckons, and shadows meet,
In leafy secrets, time feels fleet.
Each layer whispers, both new and old,
In nature's arms, our dreams unfold.

A tapestry spun of life's disguise,
In the leafy ball, the truth resides.
Unveiled, it calls for hearts to heed,
The wisdom found in every seed.

Sculpture of Shadows in Mossy Retreats

In mossy retreats where shadows play,
Nature's sculptures come out to sway.
Soft and lush, the ground does yield,
Architects of silence, a hidden field.

Twisted branches, silhouettes cast,
Echoes of stories from ages past.
Each curve and line, a tale of grace,
A testament to time's gentle pace.

Fungi flourish in emerald's embrace,
Creating a cradle, a soft resting place.
While sunlight filters, a golden beam,
Awakening visions, a waking dream.

The art of nature, raw and free,
A dance of shadows, a mystic spree.
In this retreat, we find our muse,
Inspiration blooms, and hearts infuse.

So pause awhile, breathe in the air,
In these quiet woods, let your spirit bare.
For in mossy retreats, life's stories are told,
In shadows sculpted, a wonder to behold.

Whispers of Verdant Magic

In the heart of the emerald glade,
Soft whispers of secrets laid,
Beneath the boughs where shadows play,
Nature sings, night turns to day.

Mossy beds underfoot do lie,
Where moonlight spins, the stars comply,
Gentle breezes carry tales,
Moments caught in nature's veils.

Each leaf a tome, each breeze a song,
In this realm, we all belong,
With every rustle, there's a sigh,
The forest breathes, the spirits fly.

Colors dance in dappled light,
The magic woven, pure delight,
Here whispers weave through time and space,
Embracing all in nature's grace.

So walk with me where shadows blend,
And let the verdant magic send,
A tranquil heart and open mind,
For in these woods, peace you will find.

Elves Dance in Twilight Mist

When twilight wraps the world in grace,
Elves emerge in a hidden place,
With laughter light and spirits free,
They dance through branches of the tree.

Moonbeams flicker on silken skin,
As melodies of joy begin,
A twirling flow of whispered dreams,
In silver light, the forest gleams.

Their feet brush softly on the ground,
In circles spun, the magic found,
With every leap, a story shared,
In the night air, no soul ensnared.

Through mist that swirls like spinning leaves,
Their joyous hearts the forest weaves,
Together in this twilight time,
A dance of magic, rhythm, rhyme.

So let us join in this gentle trance,
Where time dissolves in purest chance,
Step lightly now, let spirits rise,
In the twilight mist, love never dies.

The Enchanted Canopy's Laughter

Above us sways the wondrous canopy,
With laughter echoed in harmony,
Bright leaves shimmering in the sun,
A place where joy is never done.

The branches twist, the shadows play,
As creatures stir in bright array,
In every nook, a story spins,
Where beauty reigns and life begins.

Birds serenade with songs so sweet,
While blossoms sway in gentle heat,
The laughter weaves a vibrant thread,
Through every heart and every head.

Here in this haven, spirits soar,
With every giggle, life restores,
A tapestry of joy entwined,
Within the leaves, pure love we find.

So let us bask in wondrous sights,
Where canopy laughter ignites,
In the joy of nature's cheer,
Find the magic that draws us near.

Glimmers of Joy in the Swamp

In the murky depths where shadows dwell,
Glimmers of joy begin to swell,
Fireflies twinkling in night's embrace,
They guide us through this hidden place.

The croak of frogs, a rhythmic tune,
Under the watchful eye of the moon,
Whispers of water and earthy clay,
In the swamp where the heart can play.

Bulrushes sway in the cooling air,
Nature's wonders, a vibrant flare,
With every ripple, a dance unfolds,
In the swamp's tales, adventure beholds.

Beneath the surface, life abounds,
In every corner, magic surrounds,
A symphony of life so grand,
In whispers caught, we understand.

So wander deep where the wild things roam,
In the swamp, we find our home,
With glimmers of joy lighting the night,
Embrace the shadows, embrace the light.

Foliage That Sings at Twilight

Beneath the boughs, where shadows creep,
The whispers of leaves begin to speak.
A symphony soft, of gentle breeze,
Awakens the twilight, among the trees.

Crickets join in, with a rhythmic tune,
As stars ignite, beneath the moon.
Each rustle a note, a sweet refrain,
Turning the dusk into a melodic domain.

The colors fade, yet beauty remains,
Nature's choir in the dusk's soft chains.
Harmonies weave through branches wide,
In the twilight glow, where secrets hide.

As night descends with a velvet sigh,
The foliage sings, while the world slips by.
In the hush of dusk, their melodies cling,
To the heart of the night, where dreams take wing.

A dance of leaves, in the cooling air,
Twilight's embrace, a moment so rare.
Nature's own song, a celestial ring,
In the fading light, the foliage sings.

Mischief in the Verdant Hollow

In the hollow deep, where shadows play,
Squirrels and rabbits dance and sway.
Leaves rustle softly, secrets unfold,
A tale of mischief, in green and gold.

Foxes weave through glen and glade,
Chasing moonbeams, unafraid.
Whispers of fun float on gusts, sly,
As echoes of laughter drift through the sky.

Beneath the ferns, in emerald beds,
They plot their schemes, in playful threads.
A chase ensues, quick and spry,
In the hidden nook where wild things lie.

Evening light, a playful shroud,
Drapes the hollow, where spirits are loud.
Nature conspires, with a twinkle and tease,
In the verdant realm, where mischief's a breeze.

Yet, when the stars in the night appear,
The laughter fades, but magic is near.
Resting in peace, till dawn breaks free,
In the hollow of dreams, where all can be.

Raucous Revelations of the Enchanted Grove

In the grove where secrets reside,
Whispers of wonder cannot hide.
Leaves aflutter, in laughter so grand,
Nature reveals her enchanting band.

Owls hoot secrets to partners of night,
While fireflies twinkle, with delicate light.
The moon casts shadows, dancing in play,
In this magical realm, where spirits sway.

Roots intertwine like stories untold,
As the breeze carries tales, young and old.
Raucous revelations, the trees declare,
In the hush of night, filling the air.

Nature's wild chorus, a jubilant sound,
Echoes of life, in harmony found.
Each rustle a spark, igniting the dream,
In the enchanted grove, where wonders gleam.

When daybreak kisses the leafy sighs,
The grove holds its secrets, beneath the skies.
Yet still it whispers, in shadows it roves,
Raucous and wild, in the enchanted groves.

Festive Fronds in Twilight's Embrace

In twilight's embrace, where shadows bloom,
Fronds gather round, dispelling the gloom.
Dancing in rhythm, with a playful grace,
A celebration of life, in this peaceful place.

Golden hues filter through the green,
Illuminating secrets, in a vibrant sheen.
Each leaf a dancer, with joy to express,
Woven in laughter, in nature's finesse.

The chorus of crickets joins in the fun,
As stars awaken, one by one.
Frogs serenade with their gentle croak,
While night weaves magic, with every stroke.

Festive fronds sway, to the moon's sweet song,
In the heart of the forest, where dreams belong.
Together they revel, in nature's delight,
In twilight's soft clasp, all feels right.

As night deepens, this magic remains,
In whispers of leaves, where joy sustains.
A festival held, in the dimming light,
With festive fronds dancing, till the dawn bright.

Woeful Glances and Elated Twists

In the depths of sorrow's hold,
Eyes reflect what hearts have told.
Whispered tales of dreams once bright,
Now linger in the fading light.

Yet amidst the heavy gloom,
A twist of fate begins to bloom.
Laughter erupts through silent tears,
Unraveling the weight of fears.

Stars twinkle through the darkest night,
Dancing shadows, taking flight.
In glances shared, a spark ignites,
Together faced, they claim their rights.

Through sighs and smiles, worlds collide,
In tenderness, they will abide.
A journey forged in love's embrace,
In every glance, they find their place.

The Leafy Gala of the Forest Folk

In the heart of nature's weave,
Whispers swirl, and spirits cleave.
Leaves glisten under dappled sun,
Where forest folk their dance begun.

Beneath the boughs, a table spread,
With berries, nuts, and freshly bred.
Laughter rings through ancient trees,
Nature's pulse, a gentle breeze.

Elks and owls, in witness stand,
As joy unites each gentle hand.
A tapestry of song and play,
Dancing life in bright array.

The moonrise glows, their time extends,
In leafy whispers, friendship bends.
In the gala, tales unfold,
Of love and lore, both new and old.

As dawn approaches, spirits sway,
In harmony, they greet the day.
The forest folk, a sight to see,
In this leafy jubilee.

Elated Echoes in the Shady Grove

In the shade where laughter's sown,
Echoes dance on breezes blown.
Children play with hearts so free,
Their joy a sweet simplicity.

Sunlight filters through the leaves,
In each moment, magic weaves.
Birds whistle tunes of warming cheer,
Nature's orchestra, crystal clear.

Branches sway to rhythm's beat,
Footsteps light, the world feels sweet.
Every whisper, every call,
In shady groves, they have it all.

With every laugh, the shadows spin,
In this haven, joy begins.
Elated echoes in the breeze,
Promise summer's gentle ease.

As twilight drapes the sky in gold,
New stories shared, yet untold.
In the grove, a lasting trace,
Of elated hearts, a warm embrace.

The Celebration of Forgotten Shadows

In corners dim where shadows lay,
Memories dance, come out to play.
Forgotten tales of yore arise,
Beneath the cloak of starry skies.

Whispers echo through the night,
In lost reflections, sparks ignite.
A symphony of bygone dreams,
Where silence sings, and hope redeems.

Illusions fade, yet still they glow,
A haunting warmth in midnight's flow.
Each shadow holds a story's grace,
In twilight's kiss, they find their place.

The celebration swells and sways,
As moonlight channels bygone days.
Every flicker, every sound,
Invites the past to gather 'round.

So lift your glass to shadows cast,
In every heart, their echoes last.
In this celebration, let us share,
The forgotten beats, a love laid bare.

Luminous Echoes of Playful Souls

In twilight's glow, laughter sways,
Children dance in golden rays.
Whispers drift through fields of green,
Echoes of joy where dreams are seen.

With twinkling eyes, they chase the light,
Creating magic, pure delight.
In each small heart, a universe,
A symphony of love and verse.

Their carefree spirits, wild and free,
Paint the world with harmony.
In every step, a story spun,
A tapestry of life begun.

Through laughter's song, they soar above,
Bound by the wonders of their love.
Luminous echoes, sweet and clear,
Adventurous souls, forever near.

As night descends, the stars awake,
In moonlit dreams, their laughter flake.
With every shadow, secrets unfold,
Luminous hearts, brave and bold.

The Mischief of Nature's Palette

In the forest thick, colors collide,
Brushstrokes of chaos, nature's pride.
A splash of red, a dash of gold,
Whispers of stories yet untold.

The trees sway gently, secrets share,
While every leaf dances in air.
A symphony of shades and tones,
Where nature's mischief brightly shone.

Beneath the sky's vast azure hue,
Creativity blooms in every view.
A playful breeze, a charming tease,
Ticks the edges of dancing trees.

With each new dawn, colors unfold,
Their vibrant spirits, bold and gold.
In this realm where joy runs free,
Nature weaves its tapestry.

The sun dips low, a canvas pure,
As evening paints the world obscure.
In every brushstroke, laughter lies,
The mischief glows in twilight skies.

Vibrant Hues Beneath the Shaded Grove

Beneath the branches, life awakes,
Nature paints with vibrant stakes.
A palette rich where shadows play,
In whispered hues of dusk and day.

Golden rays peek through the leaves,
Each color glimmers, the heart believes.
A dance of light on emerald floor,
Mysteries whispered from the core.

Wildflowers burst in shades so bright,
Creating joy from morning's light.
Each petal sings of stories past,
In silence, beauty holds steadfast.

The gentle breeze caresses skin,
Painting life where dreams begin.
In shaded grove, where magic lies,
Vibrant hues beneath blue skies.

As twilight weaves a cloak so fine,
The colors swirl, a soft design.
In shadows deep, hearts beat and flow,
A world alive, where dreams can grow.

Whirling Spirits in Verdant Shadows

In verdant shadows, whispers call,
Spirits twirl in nature's hall.
With every gust, a dance begins,
Their laughter woven through the winds.

Mossy carpets cradle their play,
In tender hues of green and gray.
As daylight fades, they take their flight,
Whirling dreams in soft twilight.

Branches sway with gentle grace,
As spirits twirl in wild embrace.
With secrets shared from dusk till dawn,
A rhythmic pulse, a world reborn.

Through tangled roots, their laughter grows,
In hidden realms, where magic flows.
Each little spark, a vibrant glow,
In verdant shadows, spirits flow.

With every rustle, tales are spun,
In the heart of night, they come undone.
Whirling spirits in twilight kissed,
In nature's arms, they coexist.

A Serenade to the Trickster's Hideaway

In shadows deep where whispers play,
The trickster laughs, a dance, a sway.
Beneath the moon, the secrets cling,
A serenade the night will sing.

With laughter bright and mischief's charm,
He weaves his webs with silent calm.
The fireflies wink, the leaves do sway,
In the trickster's realm, all come to play.

The river hums a playful tune,
As night blooms bright beneath the moon.
With every step, a story's spun,
In shadows deep, the night is fun.

Through tangled paths where wild things roam,
He beckons all to leave their home.
With stealth and glee, he steals the night,
In that hideaway, the world feels bright.

So heed the call of laughter's song,
In trickster's hideaway, where dreams belong.
For in the dark, where wonders blend,
A serenade of joy transcends.

Cascades of Color in the Gloom

In twilight's grasp, the hues collide,
A cascade of colors, a thrilling ride.
Emerald greens and ruby reds,
In the gloom, where beauty spreads.

With whispered tones and shadows pressed,
The canvas blooms, the heart's unrest.
Sunset's brush with violet hue,
Paints a world that's fresh and new.

The echoes of a distant chime,
Entwine with dreams that drift through time.
As darkness wraps in soft embrace,
The colors swirl, a vibrant grace.

With every stroke, the night unfolds,
A tapestry of stories told.
In gentle waves, the shades do sway,
A chromatic dance through dusk to day.

So let your heart be still, and gaze,
At cascades bright through night's soft haze.
For in the gloom, where wonders be,
Life's colors dance, wild and free.

The Rhapsody of Woodland Whimsy

In the heart of woods where fairies play,
Whimsy thrives in night and day.
Mushrooms twinkle, acorns roll,
Nature's rhapsody, a playful stroll.

Among the trees, the breezes sigh,
While shadows whisper softly by.
A symphony of rustling leaves,
Where every step the heart believes.

With every brook and laughter's sound,
A tale of joy is woven round.
In tangled roots and branches high,
The woodland sings a lullaby.

Frolicsome, the creatures dart,
In whimsical dance, they share their heart.
Under the stars, dreams take flight,
In woodland rhapsody, pure delight.

So wander through this sacred land,
Where nature's magic takes your hand.
For in each moment, joy can bloom,
In woodland whimsy, dispelling gloom.

Swaying Joy in the Mossy Depths

In the mossy depths where shadows dwell,
Joy sways gently, casting a spell.
With ferns that dance, and whispers low,
Nature's grace in every flow.

Amidst the stillness, a brook's soft hum,
Calls forth the peace, where hearts succumb.
With every rustle, a secret shared,
In the depths of green, joy is declared.

The sun peeks through in dappled light,
While laughter echoes through the night.
With every heartbeat, the soul finds rest,
In nature's cradle, we are blessed.

So let the world fade from your sight,
And lose yourself in soft delight.
For in the mossy depths, you'll find,
A sway of joy that's truly kind.

So linger long, let worries cease,
In the mossy depths, discover peace.
In every breath, the world renews,
In joyful sway, where love ensues.

Gleeful Petals Beneath the Crooked Trees

Petals flutter down, so bright,
Beneath trees twisted in the light.
Whispers of spring in the gentle breeze,
Nature's gems, in crooked trees.

Colors dance on the forest floor,
Little joys we can't ignore.
Each bloom a laugh, a moment's tease,
Floating softly with perfect ease.

Sunlight kisses the petals' face,
In this enchanted, tranquil space.
Amidst the shadows, time seems to freeze,
Gleeful petals beneath the trees.

Butterflies weave through the air,
Chasing dreams without a care.
In harmony with quiet pleas,
Nature hums her melodies.

Here in this realm, by love defined,
Every heart's a little kinder.
With every rustle, every breeze,
Gleeful petals, joyful trees.

Dance of the Woodland Spirits

In twilight's glow, they come alive,
Whispering songs where shadows thrive.
Figures twirl in a soft embrace,
Nature's heartbeat sets the pace.

Leaves shimmer like a lover's dream,
Under the moon's soft silver beam.
The woodland spirits, wild and free,
Inviting all to dance with glee.

A waltz upon the dewy grass,
As time transforms, the moments pass.
Each swirl a story, lost in time,
The rhythm builds, a gentle chime.

Fires flicker, casting shadows wide,
As laughter echoes, hearts collide.
In the night's embrace, so tenderly,
These woodland spirits dance with glee.

Nature's joy in every sway,
Together lost, we drift away.
In every heartbeat, every spree,
The dance of spirits, wild and free.

Laughter Amongst the Snarled Roots

Among the roots where secrets hide,
Laughter echoes, fills the tide.
Tiny voices in the wood,
Whispers of joy, a playful brood.

Twists and turns of nature's art,
Every root holds a beating heart.
In tangled paths, we'd roam and play,
Chasing wonders through the day.

Frogs join in with croaking cheer,
Bouncing life exists right here.
In each nook, love's essence stews,
Amongst the roots, we share our views.

Bright-eyed squirrels scamper fast,
Moments fleeting, yet they last.
Through laughter's veil, we break the blues,
Sharing joy amidst the roots.

Time stretches thin, yet feels so wide,
In every path where we abide.
With cares released, life feels anew,
Laughter lifts our spirits, too.

The Sinfonia of Shimmering Canopies

Beneath the leaves, the world ignites,
In symphonies of day and night.
Soft whispers weave through branches high,
As dreams awaken in the sky.

Each ray of sun, a gentle note,
Plays on foliage, a lightened coat.
The breeze, a flute, sweet and spry,
Nature's chorus, soaring high.

Crickets chirp in rhythmic tune,
With rustling leaves beneath the moon.
Every shadow, every sigh,
Composes songs that never die.

A lullaby, sung soft and low,
Melodies from the heart do flow.
Among the branches, dreams unite,
In shimmering canopies, pure delight.

As twilight falls, the stars align,
Nature's magic, so divine.
In harmony, we find our way,
The sinfonia of night and day.

Capering Shadows Beneath the Boughs

Beneath the boughs where shadows play,
The whispers dance in light's decay.
With every rustle, tales unfold,
Of secrets kept and dreams retold.

A fleeting glimpse of spirits near,
Their laughter bright, a call to cheer.
In twilight's embrace, they twirl around,
As starlit breaths adorn the ground.

The moonlight weaves a tapestry,
Of moments lost in reverie.
Where time stands still and hearts ignite,
In capering shades of soft twilight.

Branches arch, their fingers sway,
Guiding souls that drift and play.
In nature's cradle, wild and free,
We lose ourselves in harmony.

With every shadow, dreams take flight,
In silent woods, our spirits bright.
We dance to nature's gentle song,
Beneath the boughs, where we belong.

Celestial Glow Over Marshy Glades

In marshy glades where moonbeams gleam,
A celestial glow ignites the dream.
Reflections shimmer on the lake,
A world awakened, an endless wake.

Cattails sway in gentle sighs,
Beneath the vast and starry skies.
The whispers of the night unfold,
As truth and time begin to mold.

With every breath, the magic grows,
In secret realms where silence flows.
The universe hums in perfect tune,
As shadows dance beneath the moon.

A mystery wrapped in misty air,
Each fleeting heartbeat lingers there.
Within this realm of soft design,
A celestial glow, our hearts align.

The fireflies twinkle, a fleeting spark,
Guiding wanderers through the dark.
In this embrace of night and light,
The glades whisper secrets infinite.

Revels in the Moonlit Thicket

In thickets dense, where shadows creep,
The moonlight spills, a silken seep.
With laughter low and voices high,
The revels bloom beneath the sky.

A tapestry of gleaming hues,
In small alcoves, the night ensues.
The fire crackles, embers rise,
As starlit dreams weave through the skies.

With whispered secrets, spirits sway,
In playful dance, they find their way.
The nightingale sings soft and clear,
As revelers gather, close and near.

A feast of berries, nectar, wine,
In moonlit thicket, all align.
With every bite, the laughter grows,
In fleeting moments, joy bestows.

As dawn approaches, shadows fade,
The memories linger, never laid.
With heart aflame and spirits bright,
We cherish revels of the night.

Radiant Foliage of the Faerie Realm

In the faerie realm where colors blaze,
Radiant foliage in sunlit rays.
Leaves whisper tales of olden days,
As gentle breezes dance and praise.

Petals unfurl with jeweled grace,
In vibrant shades, they find their place.
The laughter of faeries fills the air,
Enchanting hearts with dreams to share.

Amidst the blossoms, secrets hide,
In every nook, where dreams collide.
With twinkling lights and playful beams,
The foliage glows, igniting dreams.

A symphony of nature's art,
Each leaf a canvas, each stem a part.
Together they sing, a vibrant choir,
Awakening souls with sweet desire.

In this realm where magic flows,
Radiant foliage forever glows.
We wander through as time stands still,
In faerie gardens, hearts to fill.

Frolic of the Forest Spirits

In shadows deep where fairies dance,
The whispers twirl, a sweet romance.
With laughter light, the leaves do sway,
As spirits play in bright array.

Through winding paths of dusk and dawn,
Their joy resounds like an old song.
With glimmering eyes, they chase the night,
In secret groves, they ignite delight.

Beneath the stars, they sing their lore,
Of hidden paths and ancient floor.
Each step a spark, each giggle pure,
In nature's heart, they find their cure.

A symphony of rustling leaves,
The night unfolds, the magic weaves.
In every beat, a tale is spun,
The frolics end when comes the sun.

Ecstasy Amidst the Foliage

Here in the grove where shadows play,
The foliage whispers the night away.
With hearts ablaze, we sway as one,
In nature's arms, our dreams begun.

Petals scatter on the breeze,
As laughter mingles with rustling trees.
Within the green, our spirits soar,
In ecstasy, we crave for more.

Moonlight spills on our joyful chase,
Illuminating each enchanted face.
Bound by the night, no cares to bear,
Together lost, without a care.

Each touch a fire, each kiss a song,
In the tranquil woods, we both belong.
With whispers soft as the night unfurls,
In the foliage, we share our worlds.

The Goblins' Secret Revelry

Beneath the moon, where shadows creep,
The goblins gather, secrets to keep.
With mischief bright in emerald eyes,
They weave their tales beneath the skies.

Amidst the ferns and tangled roots,
Their laughter rings from hidden nooks.
With goblets raised and voices high,
In revelry, the night will fly.

Flickering lights dance through the mist,
While tunes of old, they can't resist.
With every step, they twirl and spin,
In their wild world, where dreams begin.

The fire crackles, shadows leap,
As goblin hearts in joy do sweep.
With stolen treasures, they sing along,
In secret feasts, where we all belong.

Emerald Whirlwinds of Delight

In the verdant field, where breezes sigh,
Emerald whirlwinds beckon nigh.
With every twist, the grasses sway,
In pure delight, we lose our way.

Through sunlit glades, our laughter flies,
Chasing the clouds across the skies.
Each playful gust, a joyful dance,
In nature's realm, we find romance.

The flowers bloom with vibrant grace,
As sunlight paints each happy face.
With every step, we're caught in flight,
In emerald dreams, we feel the light.

With open hearts, we roam the fields,
In the magic, our spirit yields.
To whisk us away, wild and free,
In the whirlwind's embrace, just you and me.

Textures of Joy in Goblin Hideaways

In shadows deep, where goblins play,
Bright moss and stones in disarray.
Laughter twinkles through the trees,
Where secrets sway in gentle breeze.

A quilt of leaves, in green and gold,
Tales of adventure quietly told.
Tiny treasures, trinkets bright,
Glimmer softly in the night.

The bubbling brook, a playful sound,
Echoes joy in the goblin ground.
Soft chirps and hums give life to air,
Crafting magic beyond compare.

Beneath the moon, their dreams take flight,
Dancing shadows, a wondrous sight.
Whispers of hope where laughter grows,
In hideaways, where friendship flows.

A tapestry spun of colors rare,
In goblin homes, love floats like air.
Textures of joy, a wild embrace,
In vibrant realms, their hearts find space.

The Mischief of Untamed Flora

In groves where wildflowers bloom and sigh,
Lilies and daisies reach for the sky.
With colors bold, they dance and twirl,
Whispering secrets in a floral swirl.

Vines entwine in a playful chase,
Covering paths with a laugh and grace.
Petals giggle, a bright parade,
Nature's mischief in every shade.

The wind shares tales of each flower's fate,
Of hidden wonders and paths to create.
Each leaf a canvas, each thorn a jest,
Entwined in stories, they find their rest.

Among the blooms, small creatures hide,
In mischief and mirth, they glide and slide.
The roots play tricks on the wandering feet,
Lighting the world with joy so sweet.

Oh, the glitter in the morning dew!
A sign of fun in each wild hue.
As the sun dips low, shadows align,
In the mischief of flora, all joy is divine.

Frolicsome Spirits of the Glimmering Glade

In the glen where the sunlight beams,
Frolicsome spirits dance in dreams.
With laughter bright like chimes so clear,
They weave through trees, bringing cheer.

A flicker of wings, a giggle in air,
Echoes of joy, beyond compare.
In moonlit nights, their secrets swell,
Tales of freedom, where spirits dwell.

Mirth unfolds in shadows cast,
As time slips by, so slow, so fast.
From flower to brook, they twirl and spin,
Inviting all to join within.

A tapestry of whispers shared,
Each tiny spirit, lovingly cared.
They dance through life, so light, so free,
In the glimmering glade, joy's harmony.

With every dawn, their laughter wakes,
A world alive where the heart remakes.
Frolicsome spirits, a boundless delight,
Guiding hearts through day and night.

www.ingramcontent.com/pod-product-compliance
Ingram Content Group UK Ltd.
Pitfield, Milton Keynes, MK11 3LW, UK
UKHW021537210125
4208UKWH00025B/686